Lucile Epps

D1451248

# The Life of Jesus

Adapted from the New Revised
Standard Version of the Bible

Illustrations by Dorothée Duntze

CASSELL

The Liturgical Press

Published in Great Britain by **Cassell**
Villiers House, 41/47 Strand, London WC2N 5JE

Published in the United States of America by **The Liturgical Press**
St John's Abbey, Collegeville, MN 56321

French original, illustrations © Editions du Centurion 1992
English text adapted from the New Revised Standard Version Bible
copyright and © 1989, by the Division of Christian Education
of the National Council of the Churches of Christ
in the United States of America
English editorial matter © Cassell 1993

Original edition published 1992 by Editions du Centurion, Paris as **La Vie de Jésus**

English-language edition first published 1993

British Library Cataloguing-in-Publication Data
A catalogue record for this book is available from the British Library.

Library of Congress Cataloging-in-Publication Data
Applied for.

ISBN 0-304-32885-5 (Cassell)
     0-8146-2303-4 (Liturgical)

Printed and bound in France by Bayard Presse

# Contents

# A strange visit

In her little house in Nazareth, Mary, a young Jewish girl, was preparing for her marriage to Joseph, the carpenter. Suddenly a mysterious messenger from God arrived and spoke to her. Mary was astonished.

In the sixth month the angel Gabriel was sent by God to a town in Galilee called Nazareth, to a virgin engaged to a man whose name was Joseph, of the house of David. The virgin's name was Mary.

And he came to her and said, 'Greetings, favoured one! The Lord is with you.'

But Mary was much perplexed by his words and wondered what sort of greeting this might be.

The angel said to her, 'Do not be afraid, Mary, for you have found favour with God. You will conceive in your

Luke 1:26-28, 46-55

womb and bear a son, and you will name him Jesus. He will be great, and will be called the Son of the Most High, and the Lord God will give him the throne of his ancestor David. He will reign over the house of Jacob forever, and of his kingdom there will be no end.'

Mary said to the angel, 'How can this be, since I am a virgin?'

The angel said to her, 'The Holy Spirit will come upon you, and the power of the Most High will overshadow you; so the child to be born will be holy; he will be called Son of God.

And now, your cousin Elizabeth in her old age has also conceived a son; and this is the sixth month for her who was said to be barren. For nothing will be impossible with God.'

The Mary said, 'Here am I, the servant of the Lord; let it be with me according to your word.'

Then the angel departed from her.

Mary went to visit Elizabeth and sang a song of joy:
'My soul magnifies the Lord,
and my spirit rejoices in God my Saviour,

for he has looked with favour on the lowliness
    of his servant.
    Surely, from now on all generations will call
      me blessed;
for the Mighty One has done great things for
    me;
    and holy is his name.
His mercy is for those who fear him
    from generation to generation.
He has shown strength with his arm;
    he has scattered the proud in the thoughts
      of their hearts.

He has brought down the powerful from their
    thrones,
    and lifted up the lowly;
he has filled the hungry with good things,
    and sent the rich away empty.
He has helped his servant Israel,
    in remembrance of his mercy.
according to the promise he made to our
    ancestors,
    to Abraham and to his descendants
    forever.'

# The first Christmas

Mary was expecting a baby. But before it was born, she had to
travel to Bethlehem. It was a long way to go, riding on a donkey;
so she was very tired. When she arrived, she had a baby boy.
That night the shepherds in the fields near Bethlehem saw a great light.

In that region there were shepherds living in the fields,
keeping watch over their flock by night. Then an angel of
the Lord stood before them, and the glory of the Lord
shone around them, and they were terrified.

But the angel said to them, 'Do not be afraid; for see—I
am bringing you good news of great joy for all the people:
to you is born this day in the city of David a Saviour, who
is the Messiah, the Lord. This will be a sign for you: you

Luke 2:8-20, 1, 3-7

will find a child wrapped in bands of cloth and lying in a manger.'

And suddenly there was with the angel a multitude of the heavenly host, praising God and saying,

'Glory to God in the highest heaven,
    and on earth peace among those whom he
        favours!'

This story is from the Gospel of Luke. Luke was from Syria. He was a doctor, and a friend and fellow-worker of Paul. He knew Greek very well, and had read the Gospel of Mark. He also wrote the Acts of the Apostles. He probably wrote in the years between AD 70 and 80.

When the angels had left them and gone into heaven, the shepherds said to one another, 'Let us go now to Bethlehem and see this thing that has taken place, which the Lord has told us about.'

So they hurried there and found Mary and Joseph, and the child lying in the manger. When they saw this, they made known what had been told them about this child; and all who heard it were amazed at what the shepherds told them. But Mary treasured all these words and pondered them in her heart. The shepherds returned, glorifying and praising God for all they had heard and seen, as it had been told them.

# The first Christmas

Mary and Joseph were in Bethlehem because a decree had gone out from Emperor Augustus that all the world should be registered. All went to their own towns to be registered. Joseph also went from the town of Nazareth in Galilee to Judea, to the city of David called Bethlehem, because he was descended from the house and family of David.

He went to be registered with Mary, to whom he was engaged and who was expecting a child. While they were there, the time came for her to deliver her child. And she gave birth to her firstborn son and wrapped him in bands of cloth, and laid him in a manger, because there was no place for them in the inn.

Following a star

Some time after Jesus was born, some Magi from Eastern countries arrived in Jerusalem. These were astrologers, who studied the stars to find out about important events.

In the time of King Herod, after Jesus was born in Bethlehem of Judea, wise men from the East came to Jerusalem, asking, 'Where is the child who has been born king of the Jews? For we observed his star at its rising, and have come to honour him.'

When King Herod heard this, he was frightened, and all Jerusalem with him; and calling together all the chief priests and scribes of the people, he inquired of them

Matthew 2:1-12

where the Messiah was to be born.

They told him, 'In Bethlehem of Judea; for so it has been written by the prophet:
"And you, Bethlehem, in the land of Judah,
  are by no means least among the rulers of
    Judah;
for from you shall come a ruler
  who is to shepherd my people Israel."'

Then Herod secretly called for the wise men and learned from them the exact time when the star had appeared.

Then he sent them to Bethlehem, saying, 'Go and search diligently for the child; and when you have found him, bring me word so that I may also go and honour him.'

When they had heard the king, they set out; and there, ahead of them, went the star that they had seen at its rising, until it stopped over the place where the child was. When they saw that the star had stopped, they were full of joy. On entering the house, they saw the child with Mary his mother; and they knelt down and honoured him. Then, opening their treasure chests, they offered him gifts of gold, frankincense, and myrrh. And having been warned in a dream not to return to Herod, they left for their own country by another road.

This story is from the Gospel of Matthew. The apostle Matthew was collecting taxes when Jesus called him to be one of his disciples. Matthew may not have written the whole Gospel, but he probably collected the sayings of Jesus, and these were then combined with other information, from the Gospel of Mark. It was probably written between AD 80 and 90.

# Jesus is lost

When Jesus was twelve he went to Jerusalem with his parents and a large crowd of people for the feast of the Passover. Afterwards, on the way home, Joseph and Mary thought he was with the rest of the pilgrims, but suddenly they realized that he was lost. They were very worried and rushed back to Jerusalem to look for him.

Every year Jesus' parents went to Jerusalem for the festival of the Passover. And when he was twelve years old, they went up as usual for the festival. When the festival was ended and they started to return, the boy Jesus stayed behind in Jerusalem, but his parents did not know. Assuming that he was in the group of travellers, they went a day's journey. Then they started to look for him among their relatives and friends. When they did not find him, they returned to Jerusalem to search for him. After three days they found him in the temple, sitting among the teachers, listening to them and asking them questions.

Luke 2:41-52

And all who heard him were amazed at his understanding and his answers.

When his parents saw him they were astonished; and his mother said to him. 'Child, why have you treated us like this? Look, your father and I have been searching for you in great anxiety.'

He said to them, 'Why were you searching for me? Did you not know that I must be in my Father's house?'

But they did not understand this. Then he went home with them to Nazareth, and was obedient to them. His mother treasured all these things in her heart.

And Jesus grew older and wiser.

# Jesus meets John the Baptist

Years later people started to talk about a man who was speaking to people and baptizing them in the River Jordan. He told everyone to change their lives and to work for God's justice in the world. People wondered if he was the person the prophet Isaiah had spoken about.

John went into all the region around the Jordan, proclaiming a baptism of repentance for the forgiveness of sins, as it is written in the book of the words of the prophet Isaiah, 'The voice of one crying out in the wilderness: "Prepare the way of the Lord, make his paths straight. Every valley shall be filled, and every mountain and hill shall be made low, and the crooked shall be made straight, and the rough ways made smooth; and all the world shall see the salvation of God."'

Luke 3:3-16, 18-22

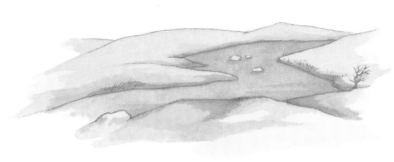

And the crowds asked him, 'What then should we do?'

In reply he said to them, 'Whoever has two coats must share with anyone who has none; and whoever has food must do likewise.'

Even tax collectors came to be baptized, and they asked him, 'Teacher, what should we do?'

He said to them, 'Collect no more than the amount prescribed for you.'

John said to the crowds that came out to be baptized by him, 'You brood of vipers! Who warned you to flee from the wrath to come? Bear fruits worthy of repentance. Do not begin to say to yourselves, "We have Abraham as our ancestor"; for I tell you, God is able from these stones to raise up children to Abraham. Even now the axe is lying at the root of the trees; every tree therefore that does not bear good fruit is cut down and thrown into the fire.'

Soldiers also asked him, 'And we, what should we do?'

He said to them, 'Do not extort money from anyone by threats or false accusation, and be satisfied with your wages.'

As the people were filled with expectation, and all were wondering about John, whether he might be the Messiah, John answered all of them by saying, 'I baptize you with water; but one who is more powerful than I is coming; I am not worthy to untie the thong of his sandals. He will baptize you with the Holy Spirit and fire.'

So he proclaimed the good news to the people. But Herod the ruler, who had been rebuked by him because of all the evil things that Herod had done, added to them all by shutting up John in prison.

Now when all the people were baptized, and when Jesus also had been baptized and was praying, the heaven was opened, and the Holy Spirit descended upon him in bodily form like a dove.

And a voice came from heaven, 'You are my Son, the Beloved; with you I am well pleased.'

# Jesus' first friends

The day after he was baptized, Jesus went to see John and his friends. When John saw him coming he said:
'Here is the Lamb of God.'
Two of John's friends decided to follow Jesus.

The next day John again was standing with two of his disciples, and as he watched Jesus walk by, he exclaimed, 'Look, here is the Lamb of God!'

The two disciples heard him say this, and they followed Jesus.

When Jesus turned and saw them following, he said to them, 'What are you looking for?'

They said to him, 'Rabbi' (which means Teacher), 'where are you staying?'

John 1:35-42 and Mark 1:16-20

He said to them, 'Come and see.'

They came and saw where he was staying, and they remained with him that day. It was about four o'clock in the afternoon. One of the two who heard John speak and followed him was Andrew, Simon Peter's brother.

He first found his brother Simon and said to him, 'We have found the Messiah' (which means Anointed).

He brought Simon to Jesus, who looked at him and said, 'You are Simon son of John. You are to be called Peter.'

Simon and his brother Andrew were casting a net into the sea — for they were fishermen.

And Jesus said to them, 'Follow me and I will make you fish for people.'

And immediately they left their nets and followed him. As he went a little farther, he saw James son of Zebedee and his brother John, who were in their boat mending the nets. Immediately he called them; and they left their father Zebedee in the boat with the hired men, and followed him.

# The first miracle

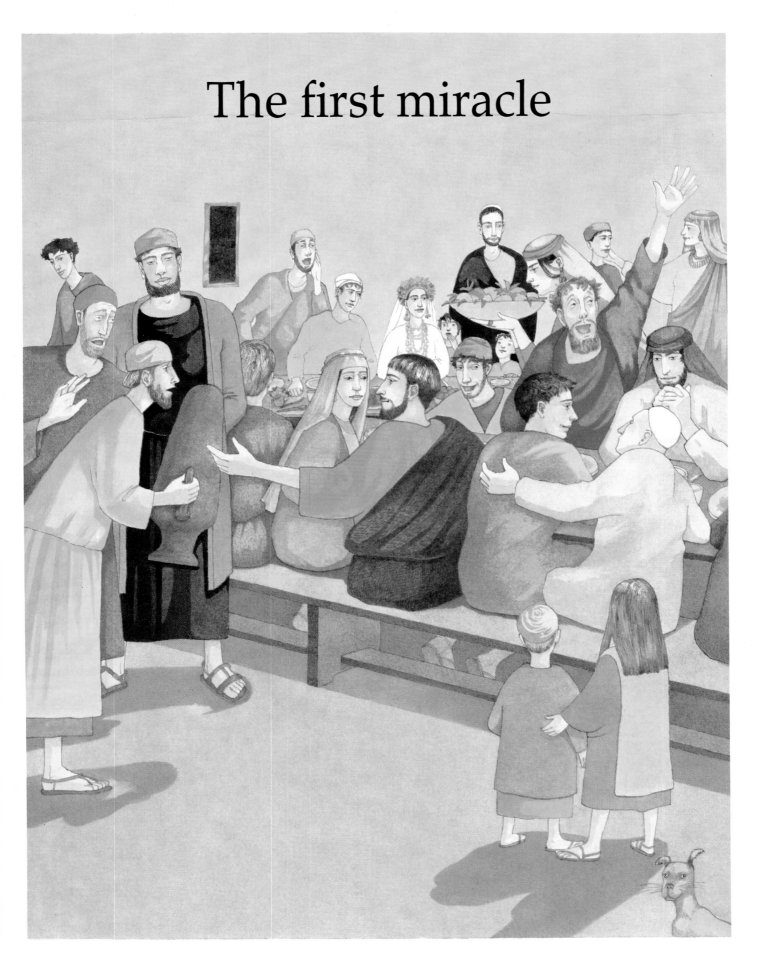

Jesus had lived near Cana for thirty years. One day
there was a great wedding there, and everyone who lived
in the area was invited. Jesus was there, and so was Mary.
During the feast Mary said to Jesus: 'They have no more wine.'
This was a disaster for the bride and groom.

One day there was a wedding in Cana of Galilee, and the
mother of Jesus was there. Jesus and his disciples had also
been invited to the wedding.

When the wine ran out, the mother of Jesus said to him,
'They have no wine.'

And Jesus said to her, 'Woman, what concern is that to
you and to me? My hour has not yet come.'

His mother said to the servants, 'Do whatever he tells
you.'

John 2:1-12

Now standing there were six stone water jars for the Jewish rites of purification, each holding twenty or thirty gallons.

Jesus said to them, 'Fill the jars with water.'

And they filled them up to the brim. He said to them, 'Now draw some out, and take it to the chief steward.'

So they took it.

This story is from the Gospel of John. John was one of the twelve disciples who went about with Jesus on his travels. The stories in this Gospel were probably written down by several people who belonged to a church founded by John. The people in this church knew the stories told by John, and had heard about Jesus' teaching from John.

When the steward tasted the water that had become wine, and did not know where it came from (though the servants who had drawn the water knew), the steward called the bridegroom and said to him, 'Everyone serves the good wine first, and then the less good wine after the guests have become drunk. But you have kept the good wine until now.'

Jesus did this, the first of his signs, in Cana of Galilee, and revealed his glory; and his disciples believed in him.

After this he went down to Capernaum with his mother, his brothers, and his disciples; and they remained there a few days.

# The woman at the well

A woman from the village of Sychar in Samaria went out
one hot day to get water from the well near the village.
A Jewish man asked her to get him some water to drink.
She was very surprised, because Jews did not speak to Samaritans.

Jesus had to go through Samaria, and he came to a
Samaritan city called Sychar, near the plot of ground that
Jacob had given to his son Joseph. Jacob's well was there,
and Jesus, tired out by his journey, was sitting by the well.
It was about noon.

John 4:4-11, 13-18, 25-30, 39-42

A Samaritan woman came to draw water, and Jesus said to her, 'Give me a drink.' (His disciples had gone to the city to buy food.)

The Samaritan woman said to him, 'How is it that you, a Jew, ask a drink of me, a woman of Samaria?' (Jews do not share things with Samaritans.)

Jesus answered her, 'If you knew the gift of God, you would ask me, and I would give you living water.'

The woman said to him, 'Sir, you have no bucket, and the well is deep. Where do you get that living water?'

Jesus said to her, 'Everyone who drinks this water will be thirsty again, but those who drink the water that I will give them will never be thirsty. The water that I will give will

become in them a spring of water gushing up to eternal life.'

The woman said to him, 'Sir, give me this water, so that I may never be thirsty or have to keep coming here to draw water.'

Jesus said to her, 'Go, call your husband, and come back.'

The woman answered him, 'I have no husband.'

Jesus said to her, 'You are right in saying, "I have no husband"; for you have had five husbands, and the one you have now is not your husband. What you have said is true!'

The woman said to him, 'I know that Messiah is coming' (who is called Christ). 'When he comes, he will proclaim all things to us.'

Jesus said to her, 'I am he, the one who is speaking to you.'

Just then his disciples came. They were astonished that he was speaking with a woman. Then the woman left her water jar and went back to the city.

She said to the people, 'Come and see a man who told me everything I have ever done! He cannot be the Messiah, can he?'

They left the city and were on their way to him.

Many Samaritans from that city believed in him because of the woman's testimony, 'He told me everything I have ever done.'

So when the Samaritans came to him, they asked him to stay with them; and he stayed there two days. And many more believed because of his word.

They said to the woman, 'It is no longer because of what you said that we believe, for we have heard for ourselves, and we know that this is truly the Saviour of the world.'

# The Roman soldier's faith

Jesus was just arriving at Capernaum when the Jews from the town asked him to help a friend of theirs: this was a centurion, an officer in the Roman army who had been kind to them and built them a synagogue. The centurion's servant was ill and he hoped Jesus could make him better.

After Jesus had finished speaking to the people, he entered Capernaum. A centurion there had a slave whom he valued highly, and who was ill and close to death. When he heard about Jesus, he sent some Jewish elders to him, asking him to come and heal his slave.

Luke 7:1-10

When they came to Jesus, they appealed to him earnestly, saying, 'He is worthy of having you do this for him, for he loves our people, and it is he who built our synagogue for us.'

And Jesus went with them, but when he was not far from the house, the centurion sent friends to say to him, 'Lord, do not trouble yourself, for I am not worthy to have you come under my roof; therefore I did not dare to come to you. But only speak the word, and let my servant be healed. For I also am a man set under authority, with soldiers under me;

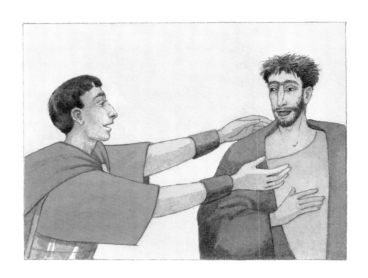

and I say to one, "Go," and he goes, and to another, "come," and he comes, and to my slave, "Do this," and the slave does it.'

When Jesus heard this he was amazed at him, and turning to the crowd that followed him, he said, 'I tell you, not even in Israel have I found such faith.'

When those who had been sent returned to the house, they found the slave in good health.

# Who is really blessed?

Crowds of people wanted Jesus to heal them. They were all asking Jesus to help. They thought that the best thing in life was to be rich and popular.
But Jesus told them that they were already blessed by God.

Jesus was standing on a level place, with many of his disciples and a great crowd of people from all Judea, Jerusalem, and the coast of Tyre and Sidon. They had come to hear him and to be healed of their diseases; and those who were troubled with unclean spirits were cured. And all in the crowd were trying to touch him, for power came out from him and healed all of them.
Then he looked up at his disciples and said:
'Blessed are you who are poor,
for yours is the kingdom of God.
'Blessed are you who are hungry now,
for you will be filled.
'Blessed are you who weep now,
for you will laugh.

Luke 6:17-30

# Who is really blessed?

'Blessed are you when people hate you, and when they exclude you, revile you, and defame you on account of the Son of Man. Rejoice in that day and leap for joy, for your reward is great in heaven; for that is what their ancestors did to the prophets.

'But woe to you who are rich,
    for you have received your consolation.
'Woe to you who are full now,
    for you will be hungry.
'Woe to you who are laughing now,
    for you will mourn and weep.

'Woe to you when all speak well of you, for that is what their ancestors did to the false prophets.

'But I say to you that listen, Love your enemies, do good to those who hate you, bless those who curse you, pray for those who abuse you. If anyone strikes you on the cheek, offer the other also; and if anyone takes away your coat give them your shirt. Give to everyone who begs from you; and if anyone takes away your goods, do not ask for them again. Do to others as you would have them do to you.'

# The lost sheep

People often spent hours listening to Jesus.
One day Jesus was talking to the very religious people,
the Pharisees, and the experts on the Scriptures, the scribes.
They wanted to know why Jesus was friendly with sinners,
and people who were always in disgrace. So Jesus told
them the story of the lost sheep.

All the tax collectors and sinners were coming near to listen to Jesus.

And the Pharisees and the scribes were grumbling and saying, 'This fellow welcomes sinners and eats with them.'

So he told them this parable: 'Which one of you, having a hundred sheep and losing one of them, does not leave the ninety-nine in the wilderness and go after the one that is lost until he finds it?

Luke 15:1-10 and John 10:7-16

'When he has found it, he lays it on his shoulders and rejoices. And when he comes home, he calls together his friends and neighbours, saying to them, "Rejoice with me, for I have found my sheep that was lost." Just so, I tell you, there will be more joy in heaven over one sinner who repents than over ninety-nine righteous persons who need no repentance.

'Or what woman having ten silver coins, if she loses one of them, does not light a lamp, sweep the house, and search carefully until she finds it? When she has found it, she calls together her friends and neighbours, saying, "Rejoice with me, for I have found the coin that I had lost." Just so, I tell you, there is joy in the presence of the angels of God over one sinner who repents.'

Again Jesus said to them, 'I tell you, I am the gate for the sheep. All who came before me are thieves and bandits; but the sheep did not listen to them. I am the gate. Whoever enters by me will be saved, and will come in and go out and find pasture. The thief comes only to steal and kill and destroy. I came that they may have life, and have it abundantly.

'I am the good shepherd. The good shepherd lays down his life for the sheep. The hired worker, who is not the shepherd and does not own the sheep, sees the wolf coming and leaves the sheep and runs away—and the wolf snatches them and scatters them. The hired worker runs away because a hired worker does not care for the sheep.

'I am the good shepherd. I know my own and my own know me, just as the Father knows me and I know the Father. And I lay down my life for the sheep. I have other sheep that do not belong to this fold. I must bring them also, and they will listen to my voice. So there will be one flock, one shepherd.'

# You judge a tree by its fruit

People were asking Jesus questions, and listening to him. Jesus was saying that a good fruit tree has good fruit, but a fruit tree with no fruit is useless. It's the same with people. You know who is good by what they do.

Jesus told this parable: 'A man had a fig tree planted in his vineyard; and he came looking for fruit on it and found none.

'So he said to the gardener, "See here! For three years I have come looking for fruit on this fig tree, and still I find none. Cut it down! Why should it be wasting the soil?"

Luke 13:6-9 and John 15:1-2, 4-17

'He replied, "Sir, let it alone for one more year, until I dig around it and put manure on it. If it bears fruit next year, well and good; but if not, you can cut it down."

'I am the true vine, and my Father is the vinegrower. He removes every branch in me that bears no fruit. Every branch that bears fruit he prunes to make it bear more fruit.

'Abide in me as I abide in you. Just as the branch cannot bear fruit by itself unless it is joined to the vine, neither can you unless you are joined to me. I am the vine, you are the branches. Those who are a part of me and I of them bear much fruit, because apart from me you can do nothing. Whoever breaks off from me is thrown away and withers; such branches are gathered, thrown into the fire, and burned.

'If you are joined to me, and my words are part of you, ask for whatever you wish, and it will be done for you. My Father is glorified by this, that you bear much fruit and become my disciples. As the Father has loved me, so I have loved you; abide in my love.

'If you keep my commandments, you will abide in my love, just as I have kept my Father's commandments and abide in his love. I have said these things to you so that my joy may be in you, and that your joy may be complete.

'This is my commandment, that you love one another as I have loved you. No one has greater love than this, to lay down one's life for one's friends. You are my friends if you do what I command you. I do not call you servants any longer, because the servant does

not know what the master is doing; but I have called you friends, because I have made known to you everything that I have heard from my Father.

'You did not choose me but I chose you. And I appointed you to go and bear fruit, fruit that will last, so that the Father will give you whatever you ask him in my name. I am giving you these commands so that you may love one another.'

# The older and younger brothers

People were still complaining that Jesus was making friends
with people who had done wrong. So Jesus told them a story about
a young man who behaved very badly and wasted all his family's money.

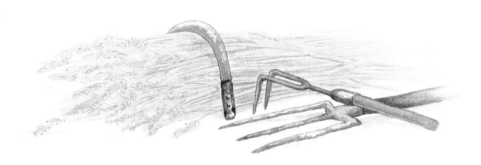

Jesus told this story: 'There was a man who had two sons.
The younger of them said to his father, "Father, give me
the share of the property that will belong to me."

'So he divided his property between them. A few days
later the younger son gathered all he had and travelled to
a distant country, and there he wasted his property in dis-
solute living. When he had spent everything, a severe
famine took place throughout that country, and he began
to be in need. So he went and hired himself out to one of
the citizens of that country, who sent him to his fields to
feed the pigs. He would gladly have filled himself with the
pods that the pigs were eating; and no one gave him anything.

Luke 15:11-32

'But when he came to himself he said, "How many of my father's hired workers have bread enough and to spare, but here I am dying of hunger! I will get up and go to my father, and I will say to him, "Father, I have sinned against heaven and before you; I am no longer worthy to be called your son; treat me like one of your hired workers."

'So he set off and went to his father. But while he was still far off, his father saw him and was filled with compassion; he ran and put his arms around him and kissed him.

'Then the son said to him, "Father, I have sinned against heaven and before you; I am no longer worthy to be called your son."

'But the father said to his slaves, "Quickly, bring out a robe—the best one—and put it on him; put a ring on his finger and sandals on his feet. And get the fatted calf and kill it, and let us eat and celebrate; for this son of mine was dead and is alive again; he was lost and is found!" And they began to celebrate.

'Now his elder son was in the field; and when he came and approached the house, he heard music and dancing. He called one of the slaves and asked what was going on.

'He replied, "Your brother has come, and your father has killed the fatted calf, because he has got him back safe and sound."

'Then the elder son became angry and refused to go in. His father came out and began to plead with him. But he answered his father, "Listen! For all these years I have been working like a slave for you, and I have never disobeyed your command; yet you have never

given me even a young goat so that I might celebrate with my friends. But when this son of yours came back, who has wasted all your property, you killed the fatted calf for him."

'Then the father said to him, "Son, you are always with me, and all that is mine is yours. But we had to celebrate and rejoice, because this brother of yours was dead and has come to life; he was lost and has been found."'

59

# The small man in the big tree

Jesus went on teaching the crowds about many sides of life, including prayer.
Then he went through Jericho on his way to Jerusalem.

'When you pray, go into your room and shut the door and pray to your Father who is in secret; and your Father who sees in secret will reward you.

'When you are praying, do not heap up empty phrases as the Gentiles do; for they think that they will be heard because of their many words. Do not be like them, for your Father knows what you need before you ask him.

'Pray then in this way:
Our Father who is in heaven,
hallowed be your name.
Your kingdom come, your will be done,
on earth as it is in heaven.
Give us this day our daily bread.
And forgive us our trespasses,
as we forgive those who trespass against us.
And lead us not into temptation,
but deliver us from evil.

Matthew 6:6-15 and Luke 19:1-10

When Jesus came to the place, he looked up and said to him, 'Zacchaeus, hurry and come down; for I must stay at your house today.'

'For if you forgive others their trespasses, your heavenly Father will also forgive you; but if you do not forgive others, neither will your Father forgive your trespasses.'

Jesus was going through Jericho. A man was there named Zacchaeus; he was a chief tax collector and was rich. He was trying to see who Jesus was, but on account of the crowd he could not, because he was too short. So he ran ahead and climbed a sycamore tree to see Jesus, because he was going to pass that way.

So Zacchaeus hurried down and was happy to welcome him.

All who saw it began to grumble and said, 'Jesus has gone to be the guest of one who is a sinner.'

Zacchaeus said to the Lord, 'Look, half of my possessions, Lord, I will give to the poor; and if I have defrauded anyone of anything, I will pay back four times as much.'

Then Jesus said to him, 'Today salvation has come to this house, because I came to seek out and to save the lost.'

# Blind Bartimaeus

When Jesus was leaving Jericho there was someone else waiting for him. Bartimaeus the blind beggar was waiting beside the road, and when he heard Jesus was going past he called out to Jesus.

As Jesus and his disciples and a large crowd were leaving Jericho, Bartimaeus son of Timaeus, a blind beggar, was sitting by the roadside.

When he heard that it was Jesus of Nazareth, he began to shout out and say, 'Jesus, Son of David, have mercy on me!'

Mark 10:46-52

# Blind Bartimaeus

This story is told in the Gospel of Mark. The name Mark is not in the Gospel itself, but the first Christians believed that it was written by John Mark, who heard many of the stories from the apostle Peter. It was probably written before AD 70, and so is the first of all the four Gospels.

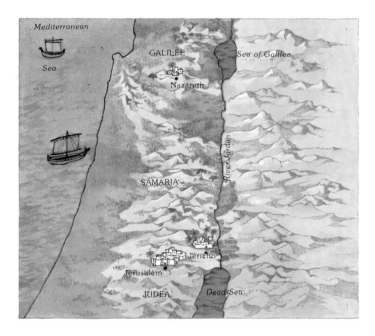

The map on the left shows where Jericho was. The map above shows the modern names of some of the countries where the first Christians took the Good News about Jesus, and where the first churches were. Mark was probably writing in Rome.

Then Jesus said to him, 'What do you want me to do for you?'

The blind man said to him, 'My teacher, let me see again.'

Jesus said to him, 'Go; your faith has made you well.'

Immediately he regained his sight and followed Jesus on the way.

Many sternly ordered him to be quiet, but he cried out even more loudly, 'Son of David, have mercy on me!'

Jesus stood still and said, 'Call him here.'

And they called the blind man, saying to him, 'Take heart; get up, he is calling you.'

So throwing off his cloak, he sprang up and came to Jesus.

# The widow's gift

Jesus often went to the temple in Jerusalem, the capital city.
And he often talked about money.
Here are some stories about the temple and
Jesus' attitude to money.

In Jerusalem Jesus entered the temple and drove out all who were selling and buying in the temple, and he over-turned the tables of the money changers and the seats of those who sold doves.

He said to them, 'It is written,
"My house shall be called a house of prayer";
   but you are making it a den of robbers.'

Matthew 21:12-17, Luke 18:18-24 and Mark 12:41-44

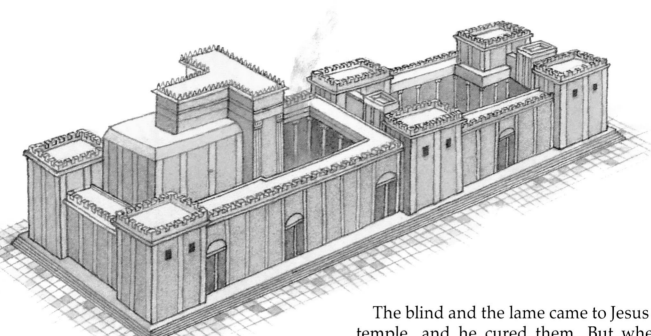

The blind and the lame came to Jesus in the temple, and he cured them. But when the chief priests and the scribes saw the amazing things that he did, and heard the children crying out in the temple, 'Hosanna to the Son of David,' they became angry and said to him, 'Do you hear what these are saying?'

Jesus said to them, 'Yes; have you never read,

"Out of the mouths of infants and nursing babies
you have prepared praise for yourself"?'

He left them, went out of the city to Bethany, and spent the night there.

A certain ruler asked him, 'Good Teacher, what must I do to inherit eternal life?'

Jesus said to him, 'Why do you call me good? No one is good but God alone. You know the commandments.'

He replied, 'I have kept all these since my youth.'

When Jesus heard this, he said to him, 'There is still one thing lacking. Sell all that you own and distribute the money to the poor, and you will have treasure in heaven; then come, follow me.'

But when he heard this, he became sad; for he was very rich.

Jesus looked at him and said, 'How hard it is for those who have wealth to enter the kingdom of God!'

Jesus sat down opposite the treasury, and watched the crowd putting money into the treasury. Many rich people put in large sums. A poor widow came and put in two small copper coins, which are worth a penny.

Then Jesus called his disciples and said to them, 'Truly I tell you, this poor widow has put in more than all those who are contributing to the treasury. For all of them have contributed out of their abundance; but she out of her poverty has put in everything she had, all she had to live on.'

# Jesus tells a secret

Jesus knew that his enemies were trying to kill him. His friends could hardly believe this. He was the friend of children, sick people, and everyone who was in trouble. How could anyone hate him?

Jesus took with him Peter and James and John, and led them up a high mountain apart, by themselves. And he was transfigured before them, and his clothes became dazzling white, such as no one on earth could bleach them. And they saw Elijah with Moses, who were talking with Jesus.

Then Peter said to Jesus, 'Rabbi, it is good for us to be here; let us make three dwellings, one for you, one for Moses, and one for Elijah.' He did

Mark 9:2-10, 30-37

As they were coming down the mountain, he ordered them to tell no one about what they had seen, until after the Son of Man had risen from the dead. So they kept the matter to themselves, questioning what this rising from the dead could mean.

They went on from there and passed through Galilee. Jesus did not want anyone to know it; for he was teaching his disciples, saying to them, 'The Son of Man is to be betrayed into human hands, and they will kill him, and three days after being killed, he will rise again.' But they did not understand what he was saying and were afraid to ask him.

Then they came to Capernaum; and when he was in the house he asked them, 'What were you arguing about on the way?'

But they were silent, for on the way they had argued with one another who was the greatest.

not know what to say, for they were terrified.

Then a cloud overshadowed them, and from the cloud there came a voice, 'This is my Son, the Beloved; listen to him!'

Suddenly when they looked around, they saw no one with them any more, but only Jesus.

He sat down, called the twelve, and said to them, 'Whoever wants to be first must be last of all and servant of all.'

Then he took a little child and put it among them; and taking it in his arms, he said to them, 'Whoever welcomes one such child in my name welcomes me, and whoever welcomes me welcomes not me but the one who sent me.'

# A king riding on a donkey

It was one week before the Passover feast, and crowds had come to Jerusalem. Jesus and his friends were on their way there too. Jesus' friends were surprised when he asked them to go and get a donkey for him to ride into the city.

When they had come near Jerusalem and had reached Bethphage, at the Mount of Olives, Jesus sent two disciples, saying to them, 'Go into the village ahead of you, and you will find a donkey tied; and a colt with her; untie them and bring them to me. If anyone says anything to you, just say this, "The Lord needs them." And he will send them immediately.'

This took place to fulfil what had been spoken through the prophet, saying,

Matthew 21:1-11

The disciples went and did as Jesus had directed them; they brought the donkey and the colt, and put their cloaks on them, and he sat on them.

A very large crowd spread their cloaks on the road, and others cut branches from the trees and spread them on the road. The

'Tell the daughter of Zion,
Look, your king is coming to you,
    humble, and mounted on a donkey,
    and on a colt, the foal of a donkey.'

crowds that went ahead of him and that fol-
lowed were shouting,
'Hosanna to the Son of David!
   Blessed is the one who comes in the name of
      the Lord!
Hosanna in the highest heaven!'

When he entered Jerusalem, the whole city
was in turmoil, asking, 'Who is this?'
   The crowds were saying, 'This is the
prophet Jesus from Nazareth in Galilee.'

# The last supper

Everyone in Jerusalem was ready for the Passover. In every house the lamps were lit. Jesus was waiting for his last supper with his friends.

Then came the day of Unleavened Bread, on which the Passover lamb had to be sacrificed. So Jesus sent Peter and John, saying, 'Go and prepare the Passover meal for us that we may eat it.'

They asked him, 'Where do you want us to make preparations for it?'

'Listen,' he said to them, 'when you have entered the city, a man carrying a jar of water will meet you; follow him into the house he enters and say to the owner of the house,

John 13:3-9, Luke 22:7-20 and Acts 2:44-47

"The teacher asks you, 'Where is the guest room, where I may eat the Passover with my disciples?'" He will show you a large room upstairs, already furnished. Make preparations for us there.'

So they went and found everything as he had told them; and they prepared the Passover meal.

And during supper Jesus, knowing that the Father had given all things into his hands, and that he had come from God and was going to God, got up from the table, took off his outer robe, and tied a towel around himself. Then he poured water into a basin and began to wash the disciples' feet and to wipe them with the towel that was tied around him. He came to Simon Peter, who said to him, 'Lord, are you going to wash my feet?'

Jesus answered, 'You do not know now what I am doing, but later you will understand.'

Peter said to him, 'You will never wash my feet.'

Jesus answered, 'Unless I wash you, you have no share with me.'

Simon Peter said to him, 'Lord, not my feet only but also my hands and my head!'

When the hour came, Jesus took his place at the table, and the apostles with him.

He said to them, 'I have eagerly desired to eat this Passover with you before I suffer; for I tell you, I will not eat it until it is fulfilled in the kingdom of God.'

Then he took a cup, and after giving thanks he said, 'Take this and divide it among yourselves; for I tell you that from now on I will not drink of the fruit of the vine until the kingdom of God comes.'

Then he took a loaf of bread, and when he had given thanks, he broke it and gave it to them, saying, 'This is my body, which is given for you. Do this in remembrance of me.'

And he did the same with the cup after supper, saying, 'This cup that is poured out for you is the new covenant in my blood.'

The first Christians shared everything. They would sell their possessions and goods and distribute the proceeds to all, as any had need. Day by day, as they spent much time together in the temple, they broke bread at home and ate their food with glad and generous hearts, praising God and having the goodwill of all the people. And day by day the Lord added to their number those who were being saved.

# Jesus is judged

After supper Jesus went with his friends to pray in the garden of Gethsemane. Suddenly a group of police came to arrest him. They took him to the Chief Priest's house for a trial.

Then the religious leaders took Jesus from the Chief Priest's house to Pilate's headquarters. It was early in the morning. They themselves did not enter the headquarters, so as to avoid ritual defilement and to be able to eat the Passover.

So Pilate went out to them and said, 'What accusation do you bring against this man?'

They answered, 'If this man were not a criminal, we

John 18:28-31, 33-38; 19:13-16

would not have handed him over to you.

Pilate said to them, 'Take him yourselves and judge him according to your law.'

They replied, 'We are not permitted to put anyone to death.'

Then Pilate entered the headquarters again, summoned Jesus, and asked him, 'Are you the King of the Jews?'

Jesus answered, 'Do you ask this on your own, or did others tell you about me?'

Pilate replied, 'I am not a Jew, am I? Your own nation and the chief priests have handed

you over to me. What have you done?'

Jesus answered, 'My kingdom is not from this world. If my kingdom were from this world, my followers would be fighting to keep me from being handed over to the Jews. But as it is, my kingdom is not from here.'

Pilate asked him, 'So you are a king?'

Jesus answered, 'You say that I am a king. For this I was born, and for this I came into the world, to testify to the truth. Everyone who belongs to the truth listens to my voice.'

Pilate asked him, 'What is truth?'

Pilate brought Jesus outside and sat on the judge's bench at a place called The Stone Pavement, or in Hebrew Gabbatha. Now it was the day of Preparation for the Passover; and it was about noon.

He said to the people, 'Here is your King!'

They cried out, 'Away with him! Away with him! Crucify him!'

Pilate asked them, 'Shall I crucify your King?'

The chief priests answered, 'We have no king but the emperor.'

Then Pilate handed Jesus over to them to be crucified.

# Jesus is put to death

The soldiers took Jesus outside the city of Jerusalem, to the hill of Golgotha, and put him on a cross, with two convicted thieves, one on each side of him.

As the soldiers went out, they came upon a man from Cyrene named Simon; they compelled this man to carry Jesus' cross. And when they came to a place called Golgotha (which means Place of a Skull), they offered Jesus wine to drink, mixed with gall; but when he tasted it, he would not drink it. And when they had crucified him, they divided his clothes among themselves by throwing dice; then they sat down there and kept watch over him. Over his head they put the charge against him, which read, 'This is Jesus, the King of the Jews.'

Matthew 27:32-40, John 19:25-27 and Mark 15:33-39

Then two bandits were crucified with him, one on his right and one on his left. Those who passed by derided him, shaking their heads and saying, 'Save yourself! If you are the Son of God, come down from the cross.'

Meanwhile, standing near the cross of Jesus were his mother, and his mother's sister, Mary the wife of Clopas, and Mary Magdalene. When Jesus saw his mother and the disciple whom he loved standing beside her, he said to his mother, 'Woman, here is your son.' Then he said to the disciple, 'Here is your mother.' And from that hour the disciple took her into his own home.

When it was noon, darkness came over the whole land until three in the afternoon. At three o'clock Jesus cried out with a loud voice, 'Eloi, Eloi, lema sabachthani?' which means, 'My God, my God, why have you forsaken me?' When some of the bystanders heard it, they said, 'Listen, he is calling for Elijah.' And someone ran, filled a sponge with sour wine, put it on a stick, and gave it to him to drink, saying, 'Wait, let us see whether Elijah will come to take him down.'

Then Jesus gave a loud cry and died. And the curtain of the temple was torn in two, from top to bottom. Now when the centurion, who stood facing him, saw that in this way he died, he said, 'Truly this man was God's Son!'

# Jesus is alive!

Jesus had died on Friday, and his friends had taken his body from the cross to a new tomb, in a garden. A huge rock had been rolled across the entrance of the tomb. But on Sunday morning . . .

On the first day of the week, at early dawn, Mary Magdalene and other women came to the tomb, taking the spices that they had prepared. They found the stone rolled away from the tomb, but when they went in, they did not find the body. While they were perplexed about this, suddenly two men in dazzling clothes stood beside them. The women were terrified and bowed their faces to the ground, but the men said to them, 'Why do you look for

Luke 24:1-12 and John 20:19-20, 24-28

they did not believe them. But Peter got up and ran to the tomb; stooping and looking in, he saw the linen cloths by themselves; then he went home, amazed at what had happened.

When it was evening on that day, the first day of the week, and the doors of the house where the disciples had met were locked for fear of the authorities, Jesus came and stood among them and said, 'Peace be with you.' After he said this, he showed them his hands and his side. Then the disciples rejoiced when they saw the Lord.

the living among the dead? He is not here, but has risen. Remember how he told you, while he was still in Galilee, that he must be handed over to sinners, and be crucified, and on the third day rise again.' Then they remembered his words, and returning from the tomb, they told all this to the eleven and to all the rest.

Now it was Mary Magdalene, Joanna, Mary the mother of James, and the other women with them who told this to the apostles. But these words seemed to them an idle tale, and

But Thomas (who was called the Twin), one of the twelve, was not with them when Jesus came. So the other disciples told him, 'We have seen the Lord'

But he said to them, 'Unless I see the mark of the nails in his hands, and put my finger in the mark of the nails and my hand in his side, I will not believe.'

A week later Jesus' disciples were again in the house, and Thomas was with them. Although the doors were shut, Jesus came and stood among them and said, 'Peace be with you.' Then he said to Thomas, 'Put your finger here and see my hands. Reach out your hand and put it in my side. Do not doubt but believe.'

Thomas answered him, 'My Lord and my God!'

# An unexpected visitor

When Jesus was arrested and put to death, most of his friends had gone off to hide. It was dangerous for them to be seen in Jerusalem. But unexpected things began to happen.

Two of the disciples were going to a village called Emmaus, about seven miles from Jerusalem, and talking with each other about all these things that had happened. While they were talking and discussing, Jesus himself came near and went with them, but their eyes were kept from recognizing him.

Luke 24:13-31

And he said to them, 'What are you discussing with each other while you walk along?' They stood still, looking sad.

Then one of them, whose name was Cleopas, answered him, 'Are you the only stranger in Jerusalem who does not know the things that have taken place there in these days?'

He asked them, 'What things?'

They replied, 'The things about Jesus of Nazareth, who was a prophet mighty in deed and word before God and all the people, and how our chief priests and leaders handed him over to be condemned to death and crucified him. But we had hoped that he was the one to redeem Israel. Yes, and besides all this, it is now the third day since these things took place.

'Moreover, some women of our group astounded us. They were at the tomb early this morning, and when they did not find his body there, they came back and told us that they had indeed seen a vision of angels who said that he was alive. Some of those who were with us went to the tomb and found it just as the women had said, but they did not see him.'

Then he said to them. 'Oh, how foolish you are, and how slow of heart to believe all that the prophets have declared! Was it not necessary that the Messiah should suffer these things and then enter into his glory?' Then beginning with Moses and all the prophets, he interpreted to them the things about himself in all the scriptures.

As they came near the village to which they were going, he walked ahead as if he were going on. But they urged him strongly, saying, 'Stay with us, because it is almost evening and the day is now nearly over.' So he went in to stay with them. When he was at the table with them, he took bread, blessed and broke it, and gave it to them. Then suddenly they recognized him; and he vanished from their sight.

# A meeting on the mountain

Jesus had spoken to his disciples after he rose from the dead, and told them to meet him in Galilee. When they were back in Galilee, returning from a night's fishing, they saw Jesus on the shore.

W hen the disciples had gone ashore, they saw a charcoal fire there, with fish on it, and bread. Jesus said to them, 'Bring some of the fish that you have just caught.' So Simon Peter went aboard and hauled the net ashore, full of large fish, a hundred and fifty-three of them; and though there were so many, the net was not torn.

John 21:9-12, 15-19 and Matthew 28:18-20

Jesus said to them, 'Come and have breakfast.'

Now none of the disciples dared to ask him, 'Who are you?' because they knew it was the Lord.

When they had finished breakfast, Jesus said to Simon Peter, 'Simon son of John, do you love me more than these?'

He said to him, 'Yes, Lord; you know that I love you.'

Jesus said to him, 'Feed my lambs.'

A second time he said to him, 'Simon son of John, do you love me?'

He said to him, 'Yes, Lord; you know that I love you.'

Jesus said to him, 'Tend my sheep.'

He said to him the third time, 'Simon son of John, do you love me?'

Peter felt hurt because he said to him the third time, 'Do you love me?' And he said to him, 'Lord, you know everything; you know that I love you.'

Jesus said to him, 'Feed my sheep. I tell you, when you were younger, you used to fasten your own belt and to go wherever you wished. But when you grow old, you will

stretch out your hands, and someone else will fasten a belt around you and take you where you do not wish to go.' (He said this to indicate the kind of death by which Peter would glorify God.) After this he said to him, 'Follow me.'

Jesus said to the disciples, 'All authority in heaven and on earth has been given to me. Go therefore and make disciples of all nations, baptizing them in the name of the Father and of the Son and of the Holy Spirit, and teaching them to obey everything that I have commanded you. And remember, I am with you always, to the end of the age.'